MW00808231

PICTURE BOOK APOLOGETICS

Whittier 2015

PITFALLS

A QUICK GUIDE TO
IDENTIFYING LOGICAL FALLACIES
FOR FAMILIES

by J.D. Camorlinga

ISBN: 0692561390

Picture Book Apologetics
Whittier, CA

PictureBookApologetics.com
YouthApologeticsNetwork.com

TABLE OF CONTENTS

* *See page 27 for an explanation of formal and informal fallacies.*

WHAT IS A LOGICAL FALLACY?*

Simply put, it's an error (innocent or not) in reasoning. Learning to identify and avoid logical pitfalls is an important part of learning to think and communicate well. This book will highlight some of the ways that fallacies fail to convey truth and crumble upon inspection. Identifying bad reasoning can protect us from making similar errors and will enable us to better discern truth. Jesus said, "Love the Lord your God with all your heart and with all your soul and with all your mind and with all your strength" (Mark 12:30). Now, let's strengthen our minds!

AD HOMINEM

against the man

This unpleasant fallacy occurs when someone doesn't address a claim, conclusion, or argument, but instead attacks the person making the claim. Making a person look bad doesn't make them wrong or prove they don't have evidence for their claim. It isn't Christ-like, either. Instead of attacking the person, address the argument.

Disagree?
That's because you stink.

Also see tu quoque (p. 9).

You're dumb for thinking that.

My anthropology teacher said it, so it MUST be true!

When something is claimed to be true simply because an authority said it is, but the person isn't actually an authority on the claim being made, the speaker has ventured into Fallacyland. If the person is an anthropology teacher, for example, they aren't an appropriate authority on evolution. Biology teacher? At least we're on the right track.

Also see genetic fallacy (p. 21).

argument from authority, argumentum ad verecundiam

APPEAL TO
INAPPROPRIATE
AUTHORITY

This fallacy is committed when a listener is directly or indirectly told there will be undesirable consequences if they disagree with the speaker. Just remember, being intimidating isn't the same as being right. Prove you have a good point by showing your reasons, not your fists.

appeal to consequences, appeal to the stick, argumentum ad baculum

APPEAL TO FORCE

APPEAL TO HYPOCRISY

tu quoque

A person commits this fallacy when, instead of addressing an argument, they point a finger back at the speaker. For example, if the speaker says "You shouldn't eat candy because it'll rot your teeth," and the listener says "I saw you eating candy during recess!" the listener may be telling the truth. However, the listener hasn't proved that candy doesn't rot your teeth or that it's a good idea to eat it. Instead of calling someone a hypocrite, show them why they're incorrect (or admit that they're right!).

Also see ad hominem (p. 6) and red herring fallacy (p. 27).

Mining is a dangerous job. You shouldn't do it!

You can't tell me! You've been a miner your whole life.

APPEAL TO IGNORANCE

argument from ignorance, argumentum ad ignorantium

This fallacy is committed when something is said to be true simply because it hasn't been proven false, or that it's false because it hasn't been proven true. Just because something isn't 100% proven doesn't mean there aren't good reasons to believe it is true or false.

No one has proved that Ultra Awesome Man isn't real, so Ultra Awesome Man must be real.

This fallacy occurs when someone argues that the truth must lie between two extremes. Here, okapi tries to keep the peace by blending the opposing truth claims of Christianity and Islam together. However, Jesus either died on the cross or He didn't, so this middle ground attempt is a logical fallacy. When two arguments are in disagreement, finding middle ground might seem easier, but that doesn't make it true.

argument from middle ground, argumentum ad temperantium

APPEAL TO MODERATION

Try my miracle cure, it'sssss natural sssso it'sss good for you.

Claiming that something is good or better just because it is natural, is a fallacy. It's the same fallacy when something is argued to be bad or worse because it is unnatural. Don't be fooled by claims that something "all natural" is superior just because it is from nature; "nature" and "natural" are unclear terms.

Let's not forget that snake venom, chiggers, and sunburns are "natural", too.

argumentum ad naturam, naturalistic fallacy

APPEAL TO NATURE

APPEAL TO PITY

appeal to sympathy, argumentum ad misericordiam

When the speaker tries to gain pity from the listener so that they will accept an argument or conclusion, this is a type of emotional appeal (others include envy, fear, hatred and pride). It doesn't prove the truth of the argument but acts as a sort of smokescreen instead.

For example, you should share this book with your friends because we worked awfully hard on it and will be so sad if you don't.

Also see red herring fallacy (p. 27).

I shouldn't have to do chores today because I've had a no-good-very-bad day.

APPEAL TO POPULARITY

argument by consensus. argumentum ad populum. authority of the many. bandwagon

When someone argues that something is right just because it's popular, they've jumped on the bandwagon and haven't made a solid argument. 100 people can be mistaken just as easily as 1 person. A large number of people in agreement about a claim does not automatically make the claim true.

9 out of 10 sheep agree that this is the proper definition of this fallacy.

Also see red herring fallacy (p. 27).

Everybody agrees this cart is headed to a greener pasture, so you should get in, too.

These plates of prophecy are true because they say they are!

If the premise and conclusion in an argument are the same, the speaker is begging the question. In other words, the conclusion is used to prove itself. For example, the Christian religion is full of bigots because it's an organization that's comprised almost entirely of intolerant people. Have we proved that it's full of bigots by saying that it's full of bigots? No. In the same way, if we say the Bible was written by God, but don't give any supporting reasons besides "because the Bible says it was written by God" we have proved nothing.

circular argument, circulus in probando, petitio principii

BEGGING THE QUESTION

Oink!
But who made God?

When something belonging to one category is placed into another category in an argument, it is a category fallacy. Here, pig is asking who made God, but since God is not a created being, asking who made Him is logically invalid. Some questions are just plain absurd.

By the way, what does "Twinkle, Twinkle, Little Star" smell like?

category error, category mistake

CATEGORY FALLACY

EQUIVOCATION

shifting definition fallacy

Equivocation happens when a word is purposefully or mistakenly misused to make a point.

For example, this chair is reserved, therefore all chairs are reserved, and we shouldn't sit in them because they are shy. Why do you insist on embarrassing chairs?!

Also see fallacy of ambiguity (p.27).

FALSE ANALOGY

weak analogy

False analogies occur when two things are said to share an attribute though they possess another attribute that makes them dissimilar.

In our example, toad says that because fake flowers have the same appearance as real flowers, they require the same care. However, since fake flowers are not living, they do not need water to stay alive. The attribute of not being alive makes the flowers and fake flowers dissimilar in a way that makes his analogy false.

Fake flowers look just like real flowers, so they need to be watered daily.

> Every time my mom makes me shower it makes the sun go down. If I don't bathe, it won't go down!

FALSE CAUSE

non causa pro causa

When poor reasoning leads the speaker to improperly infer that something causes something else, they've stumbled upon the false cause fallacy. Rhino doesn't realize that his mother is telling him to take a bath at the same time each evening, and that his bath doesn't cause the sun to set.

Also see texas sharpshooter fallacy (p. 27).

Either you let me do this, or you don't love me.

This happens when an either-or scenario is presented as the only option even though other options are available. Our hedgehog friend is saying that preventing him from jet-packing off a cliff can only mean his friend doesn't love him. It seems far more likely that a third option—that his friend does love him AND won't let him jump—is possible.

It's wise to be careful whenever an argument starts with, "if you loved me you would..." Give solid reasons why someone should agree with something instead of manipulating them with this fallacy.

black or white, false dilemma

FALSE DICHOTOMY

GENETIC FALLACY

When the veracity of a claim or idea is based on its origin, it may be a fallacy. Tempting as it may be, it can't be assumed that something is true or false based solely on its source. Sometimes untrustworthy sources can tell the truth, and sometimes the opposite is true. An old idea may still be true, relevant, or acceptable today.

Also see red herring fallacy (p. 27).

The Christmas tree has roots in paganism, as does December 25th, so celebrating Christmas is not acceptable to Jehovah.

HASTY GENERALIZATION

converse accident

This fallacy happens when the speaker jumps to conclusions with too little information. We can't properly judge the character of all monkeys based on one monkey's monkey business.

Also see false analogy (p. 18).

That monkey stole my banana,
therefore,
all monkeys are thieves!

Have you stopped stealing cookies yet?

When a question contains a presupposition, it is loaded. These are not always fallacious and depend on the context. In this case, a presupposition exists that the mouse has stolen cookies in the past. Judging by his face, it is false.

complex question, plurium interrogationum

LOADED QUESTION

No educated people believe in God.

My doctor believes in God!

No TRULY educated people believe in God.

Here, the speaker makes an assertion, and when it is challenged, they redefine the meaning of the words to avoid the contest.

For example, if we declare that "No Scotsman would ever read this book," but you happen to be a Scotsman reading our book, we would say, "Well, no TRUE Scotsman would ever read this book!"

NO TRUE SCOTSMAN

SLIPPERY SLOPE

argument of the beard

When it's argued that an action will lead to worse actions without any reasonable argument to support the progression, the speaker is on a slippery slope.

For example, why does mother owl "have" to allow owlet to skip homework every night because of one evening of grace?

Also see false cause (p. 19).

If I let you skip homework tonight, then I'll have to let you skip homework every night, and then you'll never finish college!

But I'm only in first grade!

STRAWMAN

aunt sally

When a person's argument is twisted by the speaker in a way that makes it easy to defeat, the speaker just built a strawman.

Misrepresenting an argument in order to beat it is dishonest and neither disproves nor accurately represents the original claim.

FALLACY OF AMBIGUITY

Sometimes a speaker uses vague language to mislead their audience. It is often important to define terms in a conversation. A Mormon may say they are Christian because they believe in the Trinity but their definition of the Trinity is much different than historical Christian beliefs.

RED HERRING

A red herring argument is a very general fallacy of irrelevance. It happens when someone tries to ignore the main argument by misleading or distracting the other party. Red herrings become quite popular among children at bedtime, and politicians during elections.

TEXAS SHARP-SHOOTER

This happens when data is "cherry picked" to support a conclusion, while data is ignored that conflicts with the desired conclusion.

FORMAL VS. INFORMAL FALLACIES

This book focuses on some of the **informal** fallacies you may encounter. An **informal** fallacy is an argument with a flaw in its content. As you'll see in most of the examples, the form of the argument isn't necessarily wrong but the content is. A **formal** fallacy, on the other hand, is an argument with a flaw in its form. For example:

Some dogs are brown. Spot is a dog. Therefore, Spot is brown.

Also available from Picture Book Apologetics:

PIG AND THE ACCIDENTAL OINK!
The Kalām cosmological argument

CHAMELEON'S CAN OF WORMS
Defense against relativism

'POSSUMS AND THE EMPTY TOMB
Defending the resurrection

Translations available at PictureBookApologetics.com

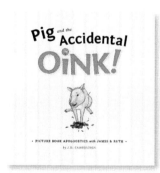 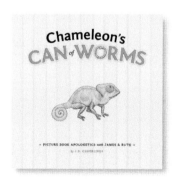 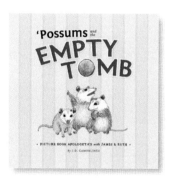 

COMING SOON: THE PROBLEM OF EVIL

Made in the USA
Las Vegas, NV
26 November 2021

35290862R00021